SCIENTISTS
AT
WORK

Engineers at Work

MONIQUE VESCIA

Britannica®
Educational Publishing

IN ASSOCIATION WITH

ROSEN
EDUCATIONAL SERVICES

Published in 2018 by Britannica Educational Publishing (a trademark of Encyclopædia Britannica, Inc.) in association with The Rosen Publishing Group, Inc.
29 East 21st Street, New York, NY 10010

Distributed exclusively by Rosen Publishing.
To see additional Britannica Educational Publishing titles, go to rosenpublishing.com.

First Edition

Britannica Educational Publishing
J.E. Luebering: Executive Director, Core Editorial
Mary Rose McCudden: Editor, Britannica Student Encyclopedia

Rosen Publishing
Nicholas Croce: Editor
Nelson Sá: Art Director
Nicole Russo-Duca: Designer
Cindy Reiman: Photography Manager
Karen Huang: Photo Researcher

Library of Congress Cataloging-in-Publication Data

Names: Vescia, Monique, author.
Title: Engineers at work / Monique Vescia.
Description: First edition. | New York : Britannica Educational Publishing in association with Rosen Educational Services, [2018] | Series: Scientists at work | Includes bibliographical references and index.
Identifiers: LCCN 2016058557| ISBN 9781680487619 (library bound : alk. paper) | ISBN 9781680487572 (pbk. : alk. paper) | ISBN 9781680487589 (6-pack : alk. paper)
Subjects: LCSH: Engineers—Juvenile literature. | Engineering—Juvenile literature. | Engineering—Vocational guidance—Juvenile literature.
Classification: LCC TA157 .V417 2018 | DDC 620.0023—dc23
LC record available at https://lccn.loc.gov/2016058557

Manufactured in the United States of America

Photo credits: Cover, p. 1 Scorrp/Shutterstock.com; p. 4 Photographer's Mate 2nd Class Johansen Laurel/U.S. Navy; p. 5 Hero Images/Getty Images; p. 6 Jung Yeon-Je/AFP/Getty Images; p. 7 Monty Rakusen/Cultura/Getty Images; p. 8 Waj/Shutterstock.com; p. 9 The Photos/Fotolia; p. 10 illusob/iStock/Thinkstock; p. 11 wi6995/Fotolia; p. 12 Cmdr. Ian C. Anderson/U.S. Navy; p. 13 NASA; p. 14 © Corbis; p. 15 Dan Kitwood/Getty Images; pp. 16, 21 © AP Images; p. 17 Science Source; p. 18 © tronixAS/Fotolia; p. 19 Chris Knapton/Science Photo Library/Getty Images; p. 20 Library of Congress, Washington, DC: Russell Lee; p. 22 Nelson Morris/Science Source/Getty Images; p. 23 George Frey/Getty Images; p. 24 © corepics/Fotolia; p. 25 Vibe Images/Fotolia; p. 26 Federal Highway Administration; p. 27 Fabrice Coffrini/AFP/Getty Images; p. 28 © Barbara Whitney; p. 29 Vladislav Gajic/Fotolia; interior pages background Richard Laschon/Shutterstock.com.

Contents

Problem Solvers on the Job

Engineers are professional problem solvers. They use their knowledge of math, chemistry, and physics to design and create solutions to challenging problems. They help make the world a better place.

Engineers build submarines and spaceships that can carry people safely to the bottom of the ocean and far out into space. They design the world's tallest buildings and machines so tiny

Some engineers design new military technologies, such as nuclear submarines and unmanned aerial vehicles (UAVs) or drones.

An engineer works on a robotic arm. Machines such as these greatly affect the lives of those who need them in countless ways.

you need a very powerful microscope in order to see them. Engineers help keep the air clean and make sure our food is safe to eat. The solutions they discover affect our lives in countless ways.

Engineers often work with other scientists. Some scientists study the world as it is. Engineers use science to create new things or to improve a product in the world. The word engineer comes from the Latin word *ingeniare,* meaning "to create."

COMPARE AND CONTRAST

Engineers and other scientists often team up. How might they solve a problem differently? How might they solve it similarly?

How Engineers Work

Engineers work in many **industries**. The largest branches of engineering include civil, mechanical, chemical, electrical, and materials engineering. Engineers from each branch solve different problems, but they also perform many of the same functions.

After identifying a problem, a team of engineers uses math and science to come up with a solution. The design process usually starts with brainstorming.

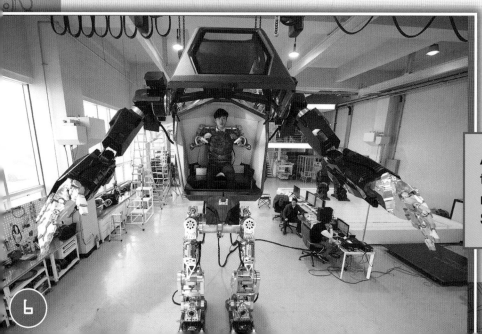

A team of engineers tests a giant manned robot in a laboratory in South Korea.

CAD software is used to make very accurate drawings of almost any object in both two and three dimensions.

Sometimes the craziest idea leads to a brilliant solution! Once the team agrees on a design, they test it. A design may fail many tests and need to be reworked and corrected multiple times. Failure is an important part of the process, as it helps engineers make improvements. Once testing is complete, the design will be produced. Eventually, the final product goes into operation.

New computer technologies have changed the ways in which engineers work. In seconds, software programs make calculations that once took humans weeks to do. Many engineers now rely on technologies such as CAD, or computer-aided design, to do their work.

Ancient Work in Today's World

Civil engineering is one of the oldest branches of engineering. It is concerned with the safe design and construction of structures. As early as 4000 B.C.E., engineers in ancient Egypt used their knowledge of math and science to design enormous tombs in honor of their rulers. Thousands of slaves worked for decades to build the mighty pyramids. These structures have survived for thousands of years and still amaze us today.

Modern civil engineers also design many massive structures, such as dams, bridges, and buildings that soar into

Of the seven wonders of the ancient world, the only surviving structures are the Egyptian pyramids of Giza.

COMPARE AND
CONTRAST

Big engineering projects have always depended on human labor. How do you think workers were treated in ancient Egypt compared to today?

A flower inspired the design of the world's tallest skyscraper, Burj Khalifa, in the city of Dubai in the United Arab Emirates.

the sky. The materials they use are often lighter and stronger than those used in the past.

Today's civil engineers try to use resources that do not damage the environment. Machines have also changed how engineers plan to get the work done. For example, giant drilling machines do what men with pickaxes once did. Chiseling a huge tunnel through a mountain now takes much less time to do.

Designs for Living

Engineering is sometimes called an invisible profession. People often do not realize how much engineering went into the ordinary objects they use every day. Many of these objects, from the cap on your toothpaste tube to the utensils in your school cafeteria, began as an idea in the brain of a mechanical engineer.

Mechanical engineers use science and math to design mechanical devices. Thrilling amusement park rides that flip you upside down through the air are fun and safe thanks to a mechanical engineer.

Engineers design today's roller coasters to provide maximum thrills while keeping riders safely in their seats.

Mechanical engineers design robots that can perform surgery or assemble automobiles. All types of engineers depend on the work of mechanical engineers. The machines and tools designed and built by mechanical engineers are used in all other branches of engineering.

Many industries rely more and more on robots rather than people to do work—as a result of advances in mechanical engineering.

THINK ABOUT IT

Which objects that you use daily do you think might have required a lot of work to engineer?

Above and Beyond

Aerospace engineers work on things that fly. They design faster jet planes, missile defense systems, and vehicles that operate in outer space. Aerospace engineers often work in teams responsible for one element of a much larger project. There are two general kinds of aerospace engineers. *Aeronautical* engineers create aircraft that travel inside Earth's atmosphere. They design, build, and test vehicles such as remote-controlled drones, airplanes, and helicopters. They use their understanding of the science of flight,

Engineers in the aerospace industry help design military aircraft, such as this fighter jet roaring over the California desert.

called aerodynamics, to make improvements to existing aircraft.

Astronautical engineers specialize in projects related to spacecraft. Neil Armstrong, the first person to walk on the moon, was an astronautical engineer, or an astronaut. Some astronautical engineers design the artificial satellites that orbit Earth. Others specialize in **avionics**.

Colonies on Mars and mind-controlled flight may sound like science fiction, but aerospace engineers are already working on these and other amazing projects.

Blast off! Many teams of aerospace engineers contributed to the successful launch of this test rocket.

Improving Life with Chemistry

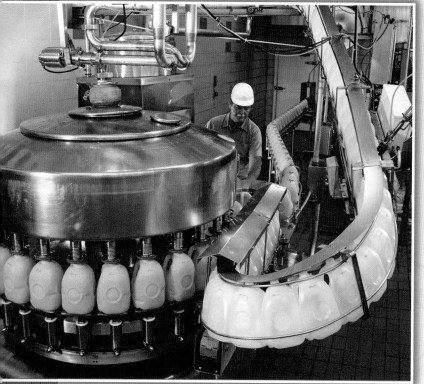

Many chemical engineers work in the food industry, where they figure out what to add to foods and beverages to preserve them.

Chemical engineers solve problems related to the use and production of chemicals. They work in many different industries, from food manufacturing and electronics to paper production. We have chemical engineers to thank for plenty of useful new products, such as microfiber fabric made from recycled plastic bottles or the process of 3D printing.

COMPARE AND CONTRAST

Check the labels on household cleaning products. Compare the ingredients listed on the earth-friendly brands with other cleaners. Which chemicals do you think are not considered harmful to the environment?

Some chemical engineers focus on why a particular chemical process affects certain materials, such as why certain materials rust while others do not. Other chemical engineers create specific products, such as environmentally friendly plastics that are biodegradable. They may develop fuel that provides a high amount of energy while burning at a slower rate. Or they may develop methods to convert seawater into drinking water.

These stacks of plastic water bottles will be recycled into other materials, including carpet and playground equipment.

Creating New Stuff

Materials engineers create new and improved types of materials. Many work in laboratories, where they develop and test their designs. Materials engineers often specialize in a particular area, such as in metals or plastics.

A team of engineers working in materials science might make a super strong glue or a cloth that can heal itself when it is torn. This branch of engineering has led to medical developments such as artificial materials that can repair tissue in the human body.

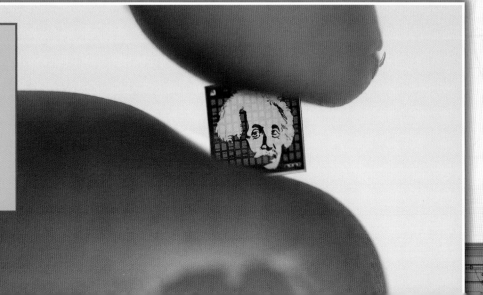

Nanotechnology is responsible for this image of Albert Einstein and hundreds of pages of Bible text fitting on a tiny chip of quartz glass.

These highly magnified particles are measured using nanometers. One nanometer is one billionth of a meter.

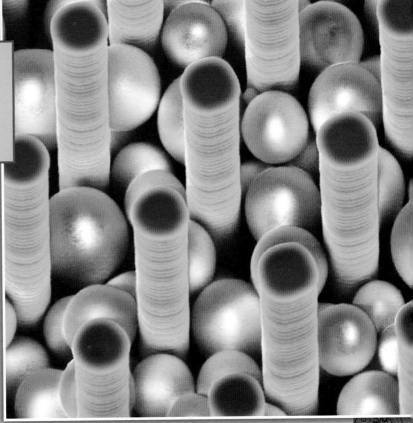

A new area in materials engineering is called nanotechnology. Engineers arrange **atoms** to build new molecules that are much smaller than what you can see with a microscope. Nanotubes are molecules used to make an incredibly strong material. Some engineers think that one day they may use nanotubes to build a huge elevator stretching all the way into outer space!

VOCABULARY

Atoms are the tiny building blocks of all matter. Atoms can be combined with other atoms to form molecules.

Medicine Meets Engineering

Biomedicine is one of the most promising new branches of engineering. Biomedical engineers work closely with doctors to design medical instruments and equipment. They design artificial limbs, hearts, and other organs. Bioengineers have even developed an artificial eye that can reverse blindness in people suffering from a certain eye disease.

This artificial hip was designed to function like a natural hip as a person walks. It is made of a strong material called titanium.

Genetically modified corn grows in a test field. Many people worry about the effect of genetically modified crops on human diets and health.

Some aspects of bioengineering are highly debated. New technologies allow humans to edit DNA, the building blocks of life. Genetic engineering has been used to create crops, such as potatoes, cotton, and corn, that repel pests. Genetic engineering may help end the existence of deadly diseases on Earth. Genetic engineering also allows some parents to select the gender and eye color of their babies. Some people worry that this new science may change what it means to be human.

THINK ABOUT IT

What if bioengineering could create a human being who would live forever? What would be some benefits and drawbacks to that?

Power and Light

The first electrical engineers channeled the awesome power of electricity safely into homes and factories. Suddenly, people could light up a room with the flick of a switch or keep food cool in an electric refrigerator.

Later, electrical engineering branched out into electronics. Electronic devices use electricity to carry or process information. Electronics engineers developed communications systems such as radio, telephone, and television. This type of engineering eventually led to the invention of the personal computer.

Before people had television sets, they would listen to radios for their world news and entertainment.

People are experimenting with ways to use robots. One day, service robots may walk your dog and make your breakfast.

We take these inventions for granted now, but they seemed magical when they first appeared. Electrical and electronic engineers are still designing incredible things. Imagine a computer keyboard you can type on by just moving your eyes or a friendship bracelet that glows a special color when a particular friend is nearby. Many different industries depend on this type of engineering.

COMPARE AND CONTRAST

In general, it is said that electrical engineers work with "heavy" current and electronic engineers work with "light" current. What might be an explanation for this?

Bits and Bytes

Computer engineering combines electrical engineering and computer science. Some computer engineers design hardware, or the different physical parts of a computer. These include microchips and circuits. They keep making these parts smaller and more efficient. Other engineers work with software, or the programs that run on personal or business computers. A program is a set of instructions that tells a computer what to do.

Artificial intelligence (AI) is a concept that some of today's computer engineers are working hard to refine. They want to build a computer that

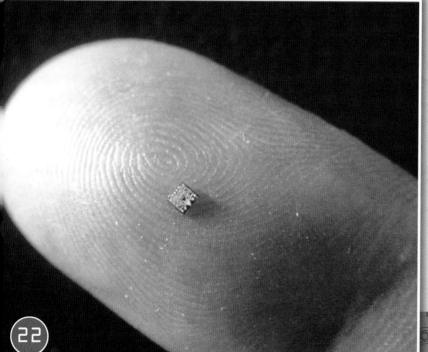

Today's microchips look tiny. However, they can have more than a billion miniature parts.

This smart thermostat programs itself. It senses when you leave the house and turns down the heat while you're away.

nest

HEAT SET TO
69
FOR THE NIGHT

thinks and learns like a human being. In the past, this idea seemed like something from science fiction, but AI is already used today in video games, cars, and banks. The helpful talking voice on a smartphone or a home speaker is one example of artificial intelligence at work, thanks to the visionary work of computer engineers.

THINK ABOUT IT

Could artificial intelligence one day be better than human intelligence? Why or why not?

Protecting the Planet

Environmental engineers help protect and improve the quality of our air, land, and water. They develop solutions for local and global environmental problems. Some work in laboratories or industrial plants. For example, a factory may hire an environmental engineer to make sure the factory does not release pollutants into the **environment**.

VOCABULARY

The environment is all of the physical surroundings on Earth, including everything living and everything nonliving.

Pollution contributes to global warming. Environmental engineers work to limit the amount of pollution that is released into our atmosphere.

Solar panels capture energy from sunlight. Solar energy is an example of renewable energy.

Environmental engineers sometimes work in the field, or travel to different sites around the world. A team of environmental engineers may design a system that converts garbage into power, or they may build a bioswale to filter pollutants out of lakes and streams. Other areas where environmental engineers are needed include air pollution control, renewable energy, hazardous waste cleanup, and wildlife protection.

Environmental engineers work hard to protect the health of our planet, for all the plants and animals that depend on it.

Three Modern-Day Engineering Marvels

Civil engineers in ancient Rome designed huge aqueducts that still stand today. Modern civil engineers also build giant structures. The Three Gorges Dam in China is the largest hydroelectric power station on Earth. Scientists say the dam is so massive that it has slowed the rotation of the planet by a tiny fraction of a second!

Engineering can change how people live. A time traveler from 1900 would wonder why everyone in today's world is staring into a small handheld rectangle, the smartphone. Thanks to the

Completed in 1936, the Hoover Dam holds back the Colorado River and supplies electricity to millions of people.

The most powerful machine on the planet is the Large Hadron Collider. Physicists watch it smash particles together in order to learn more about our universe.

computer engineers who created smartphones and Wi-Fi, people can access the internet wherever they are.

An international team of engineers built the Large Hadron Collider (LHC), the world's most powerful particle accelerator. In this circular tunnel deep beneath Earth's surface, scientists smash the tiny particles found in atoms into each other at close to the speed of light. By studying what happens when these particles collide, they hope to unlock the secrets of how the universe began.

THINK ABOUT IT

Should people interfere with nature by damming rivers or drilling tunnels through mountains? Why or why not?

Engineering a Better World

In the near future, humanity will face significant challenges. We need power to run our cities and fuel our transportation systems. The search for clean and renewable sources of energy is a top priority for engineers.

Scientists think that Earth's weather patterns are changing and that the changes will continue. As the average air temperatures near Earth's surface continue to rise, polar ice will continue to melt and sea levels will continue to rise. Civil engineers will need to protect coastal populations.

Geothermal energy is heat that comes from inside Earth. In some places, such as Iceland, the heat is close to the surface and can be easily used as an energy source.

Engineers design hydroelectric dams in order to produce electricity. Hydropower is a renewable source of energy.

Another problem for engineers to solve is that many people throughout the world do not have access to clean water to drink.

Genetic engineers hope to end fatal diseases and to create plants that can feed more people. Engineers from all branches will therefore play a role in shaping our future.

THINK ABOUT IT

What do you believe is the most important problem that future engineers will need to solve?

Glossary

AERODYNAMICS A science that studies the movement of air and the way that objects (such as airplanes or cars) move through the air.

AQUEDUCT A large bridge built to carry water across a valley.

ARTIFICIAL Made by humans.

ARTIFICIAL INTELLIGENCE (AI) The power of a machine to imitate intelligent human behavior.

BIODEGRADABLE Capable of being broken down especially into harmless products by the action of living things, such as bacteria.

BIOSWALE A patch of vegetation, made up of grass, trees, flowers, and other plants, that absorbs storm water runoff.

BRAINSTORMING A technique used to solve problems and encourage creativity in which members of a group share their ideas about a subject.

CHEMISTRY A science that deals with the composition, structure, and properties of substances and with the changes that they go through

CIRCUIT The complete path of an electrical current.

HYDROELECTRIC Relating to the production of electricity by water power.

MICROCHIP A group of tiny electronic circuits that work together on a very small piece of hard material, such as silicon.

NANOTECHNOLOGY The art of manipulating materials on an atomic or molecular scale.

PARTICLE ACCELERATOR A machine that causes atomic particles to move faster and faster.

PHYSICS A science that deals with matter and energy and their interactions.

POLLUTANT Something that makes something, such as air or water, impure and often unsafe.

RENEWABLE Able to be replaced by nature.

SPECIALIZE To focus on one subject.

WI-FI A networking technology that uses radio waves to transmit data at high speeds over short distances.

For More Information

Books

Davis, Kathryn Gibbs. *Mr. Ferris and His Wheel*. Boston, MA: Houghton Mifflin Harcourt, 2014.

Miller, Reagan. *Engineering in Our Everyday Lives*. New York, NY: Crabtree Publishing Company, 2014.

Paris, Stephanie. *Engineering Feats & Failures*. Westminster, CA: Teacher Created Materials, 2012.

Rauf, Don. *Solving Real-World Problems with Chemical Engineering*. New York, NY: Britannica Educational Publishing, 2016.

Rooney, Anne. *Aerospace Engineering and the Principles of Flight* (Engineering in Action). New York, NY: Crabtree Publishing Company, 2012.

Slingerland, Janet. *Nanotechnology* (Cutting Edge Science and Technology). Edina, MN: ABDO, 2016.

Websites

Because of the changing nature of internet links, Rosen Publishing has developed an online list of websites related to the subject of this book. This site is updated regularly. Please use this link to access the list:

http://www.rosenlinks.com/SAW/engine

Index